The Minor Prophets.ipp

God's Word to Us In Poetic Prose

by

Larry N. Locha

1

ISBN   978-0-6151-8023-6

Forward

During my quest to finish this work, I look back to the time I was first challenged. It was during our start at a Sunday Morning Bible Study, when the Adult VI Director, our teacher, Scott Meador, said that he bet I could do a little something with the Book of Daniel, poetically.

So, for the next three weeks, I set out, inspired, to completely redo the Book of Daniel into poetic prose, hence the ".ipp". I was delighted when asked to share my work during the next several weeks of study. It has been described as a "Cliff Notes" version of the text.

I am truly thankful to God for direction and guidance during the time I spent on Daniel. I then charted out to go to another prophet. I looked up Jeremiah, and was I ever so overwhelmed. I decided to give it a break. Jeremiah has 52 chapters, a lengthy work I didn't yet want to get started on. But when we started to look briefly at eight of the Minor Prophets, I decided again to give it a go. These were short books with lots of meaning. Thus the enclosed work ensued. Much insight and understanding was gained as I reworked these pieces of writing.

We are all sinners, but we want to do what is right. We all want to feel secure, but don't know exactly how to find it. But God can help us in all areas. All we need to do is accept His free gift, His peace beyond understanding, His joy and abundance. We need to get our "awe" back in awesome God.

Yet there are murderers, adulterers, molesters, cheaters, and schemers. There are those who openly sin and those who secretly sin. Sex is running wild, with internet porn, adult movies, and explicit magazines and books readily available. Theft, violence, prostitution, and corruption are things one can read about on a daily basis.

Widows, the poor, helpless and wretched need help. Are we giving it? Are we doing enough? Can we do more? We all stand in need of His loving grace. This is the case in each of these books. May God richly bless you as you read these "still-relevant" troubles and His grace.

"Ask, and it shall be given; seek, and ye shall find. Knock, and it shall be opened." (Matt.7:7)

Acknowledgements

In addition to God's mercy and guidance, I wish to thank Scott Meador and the Sunday School Class at Shearer Hills Baptist Church for their love and warmth of allowing me to share my poetic renditions of these words of God to His people.

I also extend my gratitude to Rev. (Dr.) Dowell Loftis for his inspirational and uplifting messages. God is in control and watches over all. He tells who and when things will happen. "Only trust Him" is a message all need to hear. We must live in Him and actively strive to live righteous lives.

Credit is also due to the Christian Theological Seminary, Paul Abramson, and R. Gibson (thebiblerevival.com and breadsite.org) for allowing use of various clipart images from their websites.

Finally, I thank my wife, Olga, and our three children, Daria, Alexandra, and Peter, for their love and patience during this time of revelation for me.

Dedication

To God-loving people everywhere

Themes

Hosea: Two things contrast: The love of God, and the waywardness Israel has trod. Faithful, caring, forgiving, loving for one; the other faithless, straying, sinful, rebellious and wanton. Ignorant of what God requires, Israel's pleasing Him lacks desire.

Joel: If God's people don't repent, there will be a judgment. Just like locusts bare the trees strip, God will bare the land rip. But then, God will restore and bless the people in the end.

Amos: As He is, so for righteousness He demands, but the unrighteousness and injustice are cause for reprimands, only to be restored by power and mercy of God's commands.

Obadiah: God hates what is sent, treachery and pride visited by His judgment. Brother watching brother in destruction, but also participating in the corruption. God can't sit idly by, and just wonder why.

Jonah: For all people, God His love declares, as He is in control of the forces of nature.

Micah: Demands of justice, humility, and love is from the righteous of God above.

Those persisting in rebellion, oppression
and pride will, by judgment, be denied.
Indeed, all people will be held accountable,
but God's love is undeniably always
reliable.

Nahum: Setting boundaries for nations,
destruction for any aberration. Yet, God is
good,
slow to anger, and offers good tidings for
those who trust and not fret.

Habakkuk: God has all in sight and will
do what is right. Trust is a must. His
salvation is looking through difficult times
and seek His revelation.

Zephaniah: God will judge all for their
sins. But when His people repent from
within, God lays aside judgment and
provides life's fulfillment.

Haggai: God is His people's authority and
wants to be their first priority. For the
good of God's people, provided in a
worship place, as God has promised to fill
with His glory and grace.

Zechariah: For the needs of His people,
God, Lord of all, provides for all.
Protection, prosperity, strength and grace
are given, but to know God better, they
must, by messiah, be driven.

Malachi: God hates hypocrisy and sinful livin', but those who come to Him are forgiven. Faithfulness, devotion, and obedience are His expectations, for His love and forgiveness,
as in the messiah's coming, is a demonstration.

The Book of Hosea.ipp

Hosea 1

The Lord gave messages to Hosea,
When Uzziah, Jotham, Ahaz, and
Hezekiah were kings of Judah.

The King of Israel was Jeroboam.
First the Lord spoke to Hosea, "To show
'em."

"Go and marry a prostitute, like my people
untrue to me,"
Openly committing adultery."

Hosea took Gomer as his wife,
Soon giving a son life.

The child, they named Jezreel,
God's putting an end to the independence
of Israel.

A daughter born soon, named Lo-
ruhamah.
Though God stopped showing love to
Israel, he still showed to the people of
Judah.

A second son came shortly,
And God said, "They're not my people and
I'm not their God" – name him 'Lo-ammi.'"

"Time will come when the Israel nation
Will number like beach sand in
population.

"Time will come when God can
Out of exile, bring both Judah and Israel,
and will plant his people in his land.

In that day, you see,
Brothers will be called "my people" –
'Ammi.'

"And sisters called Rahamah,
'The ones I love.'"

Hosea 2

"No longer my wife, I no longer her
husband, to account, call Israel.
Strip naked of garish make-up and
suggestive clothing, stop playing the
prostitution thrill.

"I will not love her children as my own,
As she has conceived while in adultery
prone.

"I can fence her in,
And when she can't catch her lovers, she'll
come to her senses, then.

" 'Better off,' will she say, 'to my husband
return.'
The grain, wine, and olive oil, I gave her,
she needs to learn.

But now I will the wine and her harvest
take back,
Away with the linen and clothing, leaving
you naked; I will show no slack!

The Lord said, "The annual festivals, moon
celebrations, will I end.
Punishment will come for the times
deserted me will I send.

"Incense burned to her images of Baal,
Earrings and jewelry worn, beauty to not
fail.

"But then I will win her back again,
Out of the deserts, to return home, as
when I freed her from the Egyptian land.

"The images of Baal will you forget.
All animals will not hamper, no armies will
attack; you'll live as I let.

"My wife forever, with unfailing love and
compassion, righteousness and justice will
you find.
I will be faithful to you for you to finally
know me, and I will make you mine.

"In that day," the Lord says, "rain, the
earth pleaded for
Will upon the grain, grapes and olive trees
pour."

"I will plant a crop of Israelites,
The 'Not Loved' with love will I now
highlight.

"And those regarded 'Not Mine,'
Will reply, 'You are our God, as I give love
resigned.'"

Hosea 3

"Go and get your wife again," the Lord said
to me.
Take her back, though she loves adultery.

"The Lord loves Israel still
Though people have turned to other Gods
for thrill."

For 15 pieces of silver, 5 baskets of barley
and wine,
I again made Gomer mine.

I said to her, "You must live in my house a
number of days, and stop prostituting,
No sex will you have, not even with your
husband."

This shows Israel without a king or prince
for a long time,
Without sacrifices, temple, priests or idols
sublime.

But later, the people will return to the
land their God and David's ancestors lift
Coming trembling awe to the Lord,
receiving in the last days his many great
gifts.

Hosea 4

Hear his word, O Israel! The Lord has filed
a suit against you.
"No faithfulness, no kindness, no
knowledge of God who helped Israel
through.

"Cursing, lying, stealing, adultery, murder
and violence everywhere.
Why should the land, filled with sadness,
dying, care?

"Don't pass the blame!
The more the number of priests the more
the sin. What a shame!

"When people sin, offerings to priests they
bring often fed.
But this is the way people are being led!

"Like priests, wicked,
So, then, like people, wicked.

"Alcohol and prostitution have robbed my
people of their brains.
Foolish, too, worshipping the wooden
sticks of many grains.

"With whores and prostitutes they are
sinning throughout the land.
O foolish people, you will be destroyed, for
you just don't understand.

"May Judah have such guilt avoidance,
As their worship with oaths is mere
pretense.

"Stubborn as a heifer,
Israel will be put out to pasture.

"A helpless lamb in an open field,
With men drinking and to prostitution
yield.

"A mighty wind will sweep away,
Dying in shame as to idols they pray."

" Because thou hast rejected knowledge, I will also reject thee, that thou shalt be no priest to me. — Hosea iv. 6.

Hosea 5

"Listen here you priests and leaders,
Doom is for you for misleading my
creatures.

"Led into idol worship in Mizpah and
Tobar.
As a prostitute, you have left me to abhor.

"Israel will stumble under a load of guilt
When the day comes, it'll be a heap of
rumble felt.

"Determined to worship idols, the people
of Israel will be crushed and broken,
And I will sap Judah's strength as dry rot
wood weakens.

"I will tear Israel and Judah as a lion rips
apart its prey,
And I will carry them away.

"I'll return to my place until they admit
guilt and look for me.
For as soon as trouble comes, it's me they
want to see."

Hosea 6

"Let us to the Lord return.
He will heal us now from the pieces into
which we were torn.

"Though he injured us, he will restore us
into his presence.
Oh, that we might know him. We have
learned our lessons.

"What should I do with you?
Your love disappears like morning mist,
like sunlit dew.

"Be merciful; I want you to know God.
I don't want sacrifices; more important is
the Lord's nod.

"Like Adam, my covenant is broken and
you have rebelled against me.
In Israel, horrible things do I see.

"People defiled, and other Gods you are
chasing.
For Judah, too, punishment is awaiting.

Hosea 7

"I want to heal,
But far too great are the sins of Israel.

"Samaria, with liars, and thieves and other
sinful deeds,
Has made kings glad and adulterers hot
like a baker the dough kneads.

"Kings and princes get drunk with those
making fun.
Hearts ablaze, the morning leaves no
kings or me to rely on.

"With foreign travelers they have mingled
and picked up evil ways.
I will punish them in the coming days.

"They are like half-baked cake, a graying
man who knows not
That he is nothing but a weakening blot!

"Like witless doves in the sky,
I'll throw up my net over them and bring
them down from where they fly.

"I trained them to be strong,
But they look elsewhere for help instead
from where they belong.

"They are a crooked bow,
As to death their leaders will go.

"Because of insolence toward me,
Egypt's people will laugh at them, you
see."

" And the thief cometh in."—*Hosea* vii. 1.

Hosea 8

"For covenants and laws broken, the
enemy descends. Sound the alarm!
Now Israel pleads for help, but they have
rejected what is good, and will now be
harmed.

"The people of Israel have rejected good,
Appointing kings and princes without
asking me as they should.

"Idol worship of silver and gold
Has led to their destruction to take hold.

"Samaria's calf idol, I reject.
Smashed to bits, this not-of-God object.

"The people of Israel have sold themselves
to many lovers,
But I'll gather them together, the burden
of the king to now cover.

"Many altars have been built, and laws not
followed leave you gypped.
I'll hold them accountable with
punishment, as they go back to Egypt.

"Great palaces and fortified cities built by
Israel and Judah,
But they will burn, as they have forgotten
their Maker."

Hosea 9

O people of Israel, do not rejoice for what
you do.
Your unfaithfulness to god and offerings to
other gods, is like a prostitute.

Your harvest will be too small
Toe feed all.

Grapes gathered won't satisfy,
And away from this land, you will say
goodbye.

In other lands will you live
Where the food and sacrifices are unclean
and thus not worthy to give.

"The prophets are crazy," the people
shout.
So they taunt these inspired ones,
showing only hatred throughout.

They do for the Lord God,
But the people do as when Gibeah
prophets trod.

The Lord says, "Finding you was like
finding fresh grapes in the dry desert,
But now you fro me desert.

"Though you have seen and heard,
Yet the glory of Israel will fly away like a
bird.

"The wickedness started at Gilgal,
Evil ways learned, leaders now rebel.

"There I began to hate them,
So from my land were they driven.

"Stricken, you do not listen or obey,
So from your land, wanderers, homeless,
you will stay."

Hosea 10

How prosperous Israel is, a vine loaded
with fruit.
But to foreign gods does this wealth
allude.

The hearts of the people are fickle,
The Lord will break down altars, (as with a
sickle.)

Idols will be destroyed in Beth-even,
Samaria, even Aven.
They'll cart away, crumbled for Israel's sin.

The Lord says, "A heavy yoke upon the
tender neck will I place,
As days of ease are gone, so plow the hard
ground and upon him shower
righteousness.

"Great has your wickedness gone,
When the day dawns, great will be your
destruction."

Hosea 11

"I loved Israel as a son,
Having called Him out of land, Egyptian.

"But the more I called, the more he
rebelled,
By offering sacrifices to another god, Baal.

"It is I who led;
I who fed;

"I who lifted the yoke of burden,
Leading with love and kindness cordoned.

"Since to me they refuse to return,
Off to Egypt again to learn.

"My burning anger is filled with much
wrath,
But I will not go down that destructive
path.

"Trembling they will follow the Lord some
day.
From the west, from Egypt, from Assyria,
will they come away.

"Israel shows me lies and deceit,
While faithful with God walks the Judah
feet."

Hosea 12

Though the Northern Kingdom of Israel on
the wind they feed,
Multiplying lies and violence, making
alliances with Assyria and Egypt are dirty
deeds.

Before being born, Jacob struggled with
his brother,
And with a win with an angel, God did he
bother.

He wept and pleaded for a blessing,
God spoke to him just then.

Come back to your God, with justice and
in love.
Always live confidently with dependence
on God above.

But the people are dishonest, full of lies.
These are some of the many things your
God will despise.

"I, your God, will send again
To live in tents in Egyptian land.

"I've sent prophets to warn you,
But sinning you still do."

Jacob's descendants, the Israelites, were
led out of Egypt, by a prophet,
But have bitterly provoked the Lord, their
lives to death now to forfeit.

Hosea 13

When the tribe of Ephraim spoke, others
listened.
But worshipping Baal has led to their
destruction.

They, too, will disappear like dew in the
morn
Or chaff wind blown.

"I rescued you from Egypt labor.
I, and no other, is your savior.

"I will attack you like a lion,
Leaving you crying.

"I'll rip you apart and tear
As a bear.

"You are to be destroyed,
Made null and void!

"The sins of Ephraim have been collected
and stored away.
The people of Ephraim and Samaria will
have consequences to pay.

"They will be killed by an invading army
force,
Little ones dashed to death, pregnant
women ripped open without remorse."

Hosea 14

O Israel to the Lord God return.
Tell him what you yearn:

"Forgive our sins and receive us with
grace.
So we can offer you sacrifice and praise.

"Assyria cannot save, nor can our
strength.
Idols will never be called "Our God" here
in earth beneath.

"In you alone is our mercy found."
The Lord says: "My love has no bounds.

"I'll heal you of idolatry and faithlessness.
From heaven, I'll be like dew freshness.

"O Israel, worship not idols in your land.
I'll be like a tree, always green and
growing fruit, so let the wise understand."

True and right are the Lord's paths, all,
And righteous people walk in them, while
sinners stumble and fall.

The Book of Joel.ipp

Joel 1

The message of the Lord through Joel
Son of Pethuel.

God's judgmental forewarning
Will lead to a time of mourning.

Listen all, for this has never before
happened.
Now, pass the news on to every future
generation.

A day of God is coming in a message of
hocus-focus,
Experienced by devastating locusts.

Cutting types eating every crop,
Swarming types getting all what is left on
the drop.

Hopping and stripping types, finally
settling on what is left.
To be enjoyed by tiny buds, palate, and
cleft.

Weep, for all grapes are ruined, the wine
gone.
These insects with teeth like lions leave
branches of bark, white and barren.

Priests mourn and weep with sorrow, no
grain or wine top offer.
Nor olive oil, these items having once filled
every coffer.

Weep for the loss of wheat and barley
And the fig, pomegranate, palm, apple...in
deed, all kinds of fruit tree.

Joy dried up with all this gone,
Announce a fasting time, a time to be
solemn.

Bring all to the Temple of God is the
present need
And to him, must we plead.

The Lord is on the way.
Oh, it'll be a terrible day!

Our food disappears right before our eyes
And in the House of God are many cries.

Seeds in parched land die
Right where thrown to lie.

Barns and storehouses stand empty,
While the animals moan, the cattle
wander, and the sheep bleat with misery.

Lord, help us! The fires burn away trees
and many a-pasture,
And wild animals cry out wanting some
water and nature.

Joel 2

Throughout Jerusalem, sound the
trumpet and bow the horn!
For the Day of the Lord has come to be a
thorn.

Sound the alarm on my holy mountain,
As all fear the Lord, day will be darkened.

A day of gloom,
With mighty armies across skies soaring
for the impending doom.

Fires burn out from them in every
direction.
Following them and ahead into lands as
fair as the Eden Garden.

Spreading across mountains like the
dawn,
The likes of this will never again happen
once they're gone.

Tiny horses, noise like chariots, rumbling,
And the likes of a roar of fire sweeping
fields, this mighty army has come
crumbling.

For at this dreadful sight
Fear grips all people with fright.

Fast, weep, mourn ...tear at your heart.
It's where it must all start.

Don't rip clothing in grief.
Return to the Lord your God for reprieve.

Filled with anger to have caused this
curse,
He, perhaps with your returning, won't
make it worse.

Announce again the time of fasting and
prayer.
Bring together the elders, the children and
babies from everywhere.

Let priests come mourning, and together
at the altar say
"Spare your people. Don't let us be the
object of mockery." is what they need to
pray.

Perhaps the Lord will pity his people and
will bring honor to His land.
"Look," He says, "I'll send grain, wine, and
oil, again."

"I'll remove that which makes you the
object of mockery,
Removing armies from the north and
south, to parched wastelands, and into
the seas.

"The restoration will be grand,
As the stench will rise over the land."
The Lord does things great!
Don't be afraid, just only wait.

Rains He sends are expressions of His
grace
For pastures, orchards, animals and
people should brace.

"I'll give back what the locusts you have
lost
Luscious trees, grapevines, and pastures
again will you harvest.

"Piled high to never again spoil,
Will be grain, wine and olive oil.

"All the food you will ever want will I send,
And you praising God will never end.

"You will again know I alone am your Lord
God
Never to be disgraced again as my people
upon this earth you trod.

"After the rains return again,
I'll pour my spirit upon all, even the
servant men and women.

"Wonders caused again will fill the earth,
Blood, fire and smoking pillars birth.

"The sun will be dark, the moon blood red
Before the terrible Day of the Lord again to
dread.

"Those who have this braved
To call upon the name of the Lord will be
saved.

"Those who escape upon Mount Zion,
Whom the Lord has called, will be
survivin'."

" And the floors shall be full of wheat."—*Joel* ii. 24.

Joel 3

"At the time the prosperity to Judah and
Jerusalem I restore
The armies of the world gather into
Jehoshaphat to receive judgment for what
I abhor.

"Dividing up my land, scattering my
inheritance
Making slaves of my people, girls into
trading and putting young boys into
prostitution.

"What have you against me, cities of
Philistia, Tyre and Sidon?
Revenge?! You've my silver and gold, taken
to temples, pagan.

"The people of Judah and Jerusalem, you
sold to the Greeks.
I'll bring back by selling your sons and
daughters to Arabia, I, the Lord, speaks.

"Get ready for war, train the weaklings to
be warriors, said to nations far and wide.
Come quickly, nations everywhere, gather
into the valley to be tried.

"Let all nations be called to arms, march
to the valley of Jehoshaphat
There, I, the Lord, will pronounce
judgment.

"The sickle will do the work to cut down,
For the harvest is ready, the storage vats
full of the wickedness found.

"Thousands will be waiting in the valley of
decision,
The sun and moon dark, stars no longer
shining, the Lord roars from Zion.

"Thunder from Jerusalem, the earth and
heavens will shake,
But to His people of Israel, the Lord will be
a welcoming fortress refuge without
quake.

"Then you will know I live in Zion,
My holy mountain.

"The Lord your God will be holy forever,
Allowing foreign armies to conquer it
again, never.

"The hills will flow with milk, the
mountains dripping with sweet wine,
Water will un-dry the beds of Judah; a
fountain burst, from the Lord's Temple,
divine,

"Will water the valley of acacias.
Judah will be forever, Jerusalem an
enduring oasis.

"Egypt will be a wasteland,
Edom, a wilder land.

"For upon Judah their attack,
I'll show no slack."

"In time,
I'll pardon my people for their crime.

"My home in Jerusalem will be made
With my people to stay."

"And they shall sell them to the Sabeans, to a people far off."—Joel iii. 8.

The Book of Amos.ipp

Amos 1 and 2

Amos, a shepherd, received this message
two years before the earthquake when
Uzziah was the Judah king,
And when Jeroboam II wore Israel's ring.

The Lord's voice came to him from Mt.
Zion,
(From which there will be much cryin'.)

"All the grass on Mt. Carmel withers and
dies,
The lush pastures of the shepherds dry.

"This is what the Lord has to say:
The people in various locations of the land
will experience an eventful day!

"There will be situations very dire,
As destruction occurs most often with fire.

"People have sinned again, over and over,
And now the punishment will be
uncovered.

"Damascus beat down my people in
Gilead,
For which I've said,

"Fire will be part of your destruction,
As will slavery incarceration.

"Gaza sent my people into exile
To which I'll send fires of hell,

41

"Destroying fortresses' walls,
As people and kings fall.

"Tyre broke treaties with brothers
And then sold whole villages into slavery
to others.

"Edom chased Israeli relatives with swords
and unrelenting anger.
Now fire will be sent down to danger.

"Ammon did cruel crimes during a war,
But fire will come as a mighty storm, for
sure.

"Moab desecrated Edom's king's tomb.
Thus a fire for slaughtering does loom.

"Judah, now, has rejected laws and its
people have been led astray.
But fire will I send down and destroy
fortresses where they lay.

"Israel has perverted and denied justice,
sold slaves, committed adultery, and did
form many steal,
And now with God must deal.

"You won't be the fastest, bravest, or the
strongest.
Nor will you be able to run the longest.

"You have not thought of what I do.
All the troubles, out of Egypt I've helped
you escape or work through.

"To the Nazirites and my prophets, you
say stop the croakin'.
I will not forget the punishment due. I, the
Lord, have spoken."

"Amos, who was among the herdsmen of
Tekoa."—Amos i. 1.

Amos 3

To this message of the Lord must you
listen.
"Of all the families on earth, I chose you.
Thus, must I punish you for every sin..

Does a bird ever get caught in a crate
When that trap has no bait?

Disaster comes to cities as the Lord
planned it,
"But a warning is given through my
servant prophets.

"An enemy will rise to shatter defenses,
Plundering all fortresses.

"Like a shepherd from a lion's mouth a
sheep to rescue,
So will it be with Samaria filled with Israel.

"Pagan altars at Bethel will fall,
As will houses of the wealthy, beautiful."

Amos 4

"Fat cows" of Samaria, listen, you women
who oppress the poor and crush the
needy.
You who always ask for another drink,
"will be hooked like fish and away be
reeled.

"Keep offering sacrifices to idols, each
morn,
And tithe like it should be done.

"I brought hunger and famine to every
town,
But still you look upon me with a frown.

"I controlled the rain and where it fell.
I struck your farms with mildew and
locusts, but you still couldn't tell.

"I sent plagues and wars to slaughter your
own men,
But you still didn't return to me, then.

"Your cities I destroyed,
But still you stand there null and void!

"Therefore, upon you will be further
dealings.
Prepare to meet your God and his
feelings."

He made the mountains, stirs the winds,
and turns out the light without shame.
The Lord God Almighty is his name!

Amos 5

Listen, ears ring.
As this song I sing:

"Virgin Israel, fallen, never to rise again.
With none to raise her up, on the ground,
she lies forsaken."

The Sovereign Lord says: "Each time you
send out battling men,
Only one-tenth will return home again."

Come back and live; otherwise, he'll roar
through like a fire.
Worship not idols, you're wicked, twisting
justice, a righteousness and fair play liar.

He created the stars, turns day to night,
and makes the oceans rain.
And with blinding speed, he can take
these back again.

Honest traders you hate; you trample the
poor, and steal.
You'll never drink good wine. Good people
keep quiet, this time is evil!

Hate evil and love what is right!
Perhaps the Lord God will have mercy on
those in his sight.

The Lord says: "Crying will be in all public
places and streets,
Professional mourners to help you weep.

"These professionals should you summon,
Wailing in every vineyard, for I'll destroy
them. I, the Lord, have spoken."

"They take a bribe, and they turn aside the poor in the gate."—*Amos* v. 12.

Amos 6

You lounge in your chair,
Like you just don't care.

This happened with many other cities.
Now, they're a part of ancient histories.

You don't even think about possible
disaster,
But doing only brings about that judgment
faster.

Sprawled around, eating lamb chops,
While your mind upon nothingness props.

Thus, as captives will you first to be sent,
As the revelry energy of yours is spent.

The Lord says, "I despise the pride and
false glory.
I'll give the city and all into the slavery
worry.

"Into poison you have made the sweet fruit
of righteousness,
All conquests made were done not of just
your strength, power and uprightness.

"I'm about to send
An enemy who will oppress you bitterly
throughout your land."

Amos 7

In my vision it was seen,
A vast swarm of locusts eating all
harvested that was green.

I said, "Please, forgive your people. We
won't survive, for we are a small nation."
The Lord relented to not fulfill this vision
of devastation.

Another vision did the Sovereign Lord
show me,
A great fire burning up the depths of the
sea.

"We are only a small nation," I told the
lord again.
The Lord turned from his intended plan.

Then another vision he showed me, the
Lord standing by a wall.
A plumb line to see it straight: all
punishment will not be ignored, as pagan
shrines, temples, and Jeroboam's dynasty
will fall.

Amaziah had heard what Amos was
saying,
And went to King Jeroboam without
delaying.

Orders came back to Amos,
"Go back to Judah and stop prophesying,
especially where the royal sanctuary is."

Amos replied: "I'm just a shepherd, never
trained as a pro,
But God called and told me where to go.

It's his people in Israel he wants to listen,
But you say 'Against Israel, stop the
preachin'!'"

"Because you refused to listen,
Your wife will go into prostitution.

"Your sons and daughters will be killed,
divided will be your land.
The people of Israel will become exile
captives far from their homeland."

"Go, flee away into the land of Judah . . . and prophesy there."—Amos vii. 12.

51

Amos 8

Another vision did I see.
"Ripe fruit in a basket," I answered after
the Lord asked me.

The Lord says: "The fruit are my people,
Ripe for punishment, those in Israel.

"I won't delay again,
The sounds will turn from singing to
wailing.

"Dead bodies will be throughout.
Only in the city silence will they be carried
out.

"You trample the needy and rob the poor,
Use dishonest scales in your store.

"You can't wait for the Sabbath to end,
So you can quickly turn to cheating again.

"I will not forget what has been done, the
earth trembling and people mourn.
The land and time, river floods and nights
and day, will I see tuned around and torn.

"A famine will come to the land.
Not the kind of starvation.

"It'll be a time of searching,
For God's word will the people everywhere
be thirsting.

"Staggering sea to sea
To find me.

"Those continuing to worship and swear
by every idol
Will fall down, forever idle."

Amos 9

I then saw a vision of the Lord beside the
altar.
Said He, "Strike the Temple columns,
shake the foundation, crashing to the
ground, with survivors left for the
battlefield slaughter.

"No matter where they go I will capture
and destroy them,
To the place of the dead, to the heavens,
or to the depths of the sea where the great
serpent will swim.

"The Lord controls all things, in his name,
Drawing water up to the heavens to let it
pour as rain.

"Do you Israelites think you're more
important than another?
Having brought you out of Egypt, have I
not done much for others?

"Yet I watch the sinful nation,
As I will uproot and spread its people
across creation.

"I will never completely destroy you,
But only have other nations persecute.

"By the sword will sinners die,
All those saying, 'Nothing bad will come
by.'"

"In that day, I'll restore the fallen
kingdom,
Rebuild walls, restore glory, and let Israel
possess what's left of Edom.

"With hills of Israel dripping with sweet
wine, grain and grapes will grow faster
than they can be picked,
And I'll bring back my exiled people from
where they've been kicked.

"I'll firmly plant them in this land given
And they'll never again be uprooted and
away driven."

The Book of Obadiah.ipp

"And cast lots upon Jerusalem."—*Obadiah* i. 11.

Obadiah

Revealed from the Sovereign Lord to
Obadiah concerning the fate to come,
The Lord in the vision stating, "Get ready,
assemble armies, and attack Edom.

"I will cut you down, though your
fortresses are in the sky.
Your proud boast, 'Who can reach us in
the mountains so high?'

"High as eagles now, in the stars nesting.
But I have spoken, you will crash down,
leaving many a-guessing.

"Unlike thieves, who may not always take
all,
Your enemies, though, will see to your
complete demise and fall.

"All of Edom will be scoured and looted,
Every treasure found by all enemies
together in cahoots.

"Former friends and allies will against you
turn
Promising peace, but plotting and
trapping, your land to pillage and burn.

"Everyone with wisdom and
understanding will be destroyed.
The mightiest will be terrified, but they,
too, will become null and void.

"'Why?'
Is this your cry?

"Because of the violence done to relatives
in Israel.
The needy ones deserted...the ones you
help fell!

"You stood beside, lifting not a finger to
help against this,
Acting, instead, like enemies, this
something amiss.

"You gloat as to distant lands relatives
were sent
You rejoiced through the misfortune they
went.

"You crowed over them as they suffered
disasters
You rejoiced destruction, help capturing
and killing, like you were their masters.

"The day nears when
 I will judge every godless nation.

"Those doing evil deeds
Will be haunted back, indeed.

"Just as you swallowed up my people of
my holy mountain, leaving them is misery,
So will your nation be devoured and
disappear from existence and history."

"Jerusalem will be the holy place
To which people will come to embrace.

"It will be there they will have chance
To receive their inheritance.
"Israel will be raging with fire
With Edom the place of its desire.

"I will not leave one,
For I, the Lord, has spoken.

"Then my people in Negev
Will occupy the mountains of Edom, and
what is left.

"And those of the foothills of Judah,
Will possess the plains of Philistine and
the fields of Ephraim and Samaria.

"The people of Benjamin will occupy the
Gilead land,
While the exiles of Israel return to the
coast, Phoenician.

"The captives of Jerusalem exiled north to
Narephath will return to Negev to resettle,
With deliverers going to Mt. Zion, the
mountains of Edom, over which to rule
and mettle.

"And this the final thing:
The Lord himself will be king."

The Book of Jonah.ipp

Jonah 1

The Lord's message to Jonah, son of
Amittai.
"Get up, go to Nineveh, announcing
judgment to the wicked people," as to
wonder why.

But Jonah went the other way instead,
eventually a ship did he board.
He thought having bought the ticket
would be escape from the Lord.

A violent storm did suddenly from the
Lord come,
As the ship sailed along.

Sailors shouted to gods and threw things
overboard
To lighten the boat to avoid being
wrecklessly shored.

Jonah was sad, asleep in the ship's hold,
When the captain went below to him told,

"How can you sleep at a time like this?
Pray to your god to save our lives, our
deepest wish."

To see who offended god, the crew cast
lots,
When Jonah lost the toss.

"What have you done?" was the demand.
"Who are you, from what land?"

"I am Hebrew and worship the god of
heaven," Jonah said.
"It is from him I fled."

"Why? What should be done to you to stop
the storm?" they groaned.
Said Jonah, "Into the sea should I be
thrown."

"I know the fault is with me,
So shall I go, into the sea."

The sailors tried to row to shore instead.
But the storm increased intensity, so to
god they pled.

"Don't let us die for this man's sin.
Though not our fault, you have the storm
for your own reason."

They picked up Jonah and threw him into
the sea,
And became awestruck by the power of
the Lord's decree.

The storm at once stopped,
And the crew offered sacrifices and vowed
against him to prop.
A great fish did Jonah swallow
For three days and nights did he live with
the Lords, hallowed.

Jonah 2

I then prayed from inside the fish.
I said, "I cried out in my great troubles,
and he answered my wish."

From the world of the dead did I call,
Thrown into the ocean depths, beneath
stormy seas did I fall.

From your presence was I driven.
Said I, "How will I see your Temple again?"

Under the waves I sank with death near.
Waters closed in around, seaweed
entangled my head and ears.

I was locked out of life and imprisoned
with the dead.
But you, O Lord, you snatched me from
death, from what I dread.

When hope was lost and I was crying,
solely,
My prayer went to your Temple, holy.

Worshippers of false gods don't accept
your mercies,
But I'll sacrifice with praise songs and
fulfilled vows for your courtesies.

My salvation is from you alone.
As the Lord had me to the beach spit up
and blown.

Jonah 3

To Judah and Jerusalem a second time
did the Lord speak,
"Get up and go to Nineveh, and deliver the
judgment message as to what I seek."

Jonah obeyed the command and to
Nineveh went,
And to the people to deliver the message
sent.

Nineveh will be destroyed in 40 days.
The people believed God's word, wore
sackcloth, and fasted, leaving food where
it lay.

The king took off his role and sashes,
He dressed in sackcloth, and sat atop the
ashes.

A decree throughout the city was worth
passing:
"Requiring the wearing of sackcloth,
praying, and complete populous fasting.

"All evil ways must come to a stop,
The violence upon others dropped.

"Perhaps upon us God will have pity,
To hold back his anger, deity."

When God saw the stopping of evil ways,
He had mercy, and let them live on many
more days.

Jonah 4

Jonah was filled with anger
Because the Lord had freed the people
from danger.

"Didn't I say, 'Lord, that you would do
this?
A reason I left and ran away from
Tarshish.'"

You are compassionate and gracious, slow
to anger and filled with love unfailing.
I knew you could cancel your destruction
plans, leaving the people not wailing.

I'd rather be dead
Because nothing has happened as I said.

The Lord replied, "Is it right?
For you to have such slight?"

Jonah went to find shade in the city's east
end.
But God arranged for a leafy plant to grow
there then.

The plant, soon with spreading broad
leaves to the sky
Allowed shading from the sun. This eased
his discomforting cry.

God prepared a worm
Which ate the plant's stem through which
it squirmed.

The plant withered and died.
The sun grew hot, and upon Jonah the
wind blew, fried.

Jonah wished death,
"Surely, life is better with a last breath."

"Is it right to be angry because the plant
died?' asked the Lord.
"Yes, Jonah said, "have you not heard?"

The Lord answered, "For the plant, you felt
nothing, as it is short-lived to only die.
But Nineveh, with 120,000 people in
darkness, so why can't I cry?

"Shouldn't I feel sorry and have pity
For this great city?"

"Jonah upon the dry land." —Jonah ii. 10.

The Book of Micah.ipp

Micah 1

During the reigns of Judah kings, Jotham,
Ahaz, and Hezekiah,
Visions from the Lord came to Micah.

Listen all peoples of the world. Attention!
The Sovereign Lord speaks. He leaves the
throne in heaven and comes to earth. It is
His intention.

Why? The sins and rebellion of Israel and
Judah rattle.
Blame for Israel's rebellion, Samaria; the
center of idolatry, Jerusalem, its capital!

"I, the Lord, will make a heap of rubble
out of Samaria.
Streets will be plowed up for vineyards;
the stones of the walls will be rolled into
the valley; I will have effect in the area.

"Carved images will I smash to pieces,
Sacred treasures burned; it all ceases."

Of this I mourn and lament.
Naked and barefoot will I walk around, the
people's wound is in cement.

Don't tell your enemies of Gath,
Don't cry of this wrath.

You of Beth-leaphrah, roll in dust to show
anguish and despair.

And go as captives, naked and ashamed,
you people of Shaphir.

People of Zaanan come not outside the
walls,
And the people of Beth-ezel mourn as the
city away falls.

People of Maroth wait for relief,
For judgment awaits Jerusalem with only
bitterness and grief.

People of Lachish use chariots to flee
Into sin you led Jerusalem, for you were
the first city

To follow Israel into sin.
A farewell gift to Moresheth-gath send.

There's no hope top save it.
The town of Aczib deceived kings of Israel
for promises not kept.

People of Mareshah town
A new conqueror over you will be found.

"The leaders of Israel will go to Adullam.
Weep people of Judah; Shave your heads
in sorrow; Snatchers of your beloved
children will come.

"You'll never see them again,
As your little ones are taken to distant
lands.

Micah 2

Thinking up plans while at night you like
awake.
Scheming ideas as wicked as a snake.

Wanting a piece of land, taken by fraud or
violence.
With you around nothing is safe, family or
inheritance.

But the Lord says: "Evil for evil, I will
defeat,
Leaving nothing to ever again walk
proudly in the street.

"Your enemies will make fun and sing a
song,
Setting your boundaries, telling you where
you belong.

"Don't say such things." The people say.
"Such disasters will never come our way."

Should you talk like that, O family of
Israel?
But my words are real!

You rise against me this very hour.
But if you do what is right, I'd show my
loving power.

You steal from others whom trusted in
you,
Evicted women from homes, stripped
children of God-given rights, through and
through.

Up and go! This is no longer your land and
home.
Now filled with sin and ruin, you now are
the world to roam!

Suppose a prophet preached "joys of wine
and drink.
That's the kind you like and want, I think.

"Oh, someday as in times old
I'll gather you together like sheep in a fold.

"Your land will again have the noisy
crowds of many a-smile.
A leader will break out and lead you out of
exile.

"The Lord himself will and guide
To your land through gates that did hide."

Micah 3

Listen Israel's leaders, you're suppose to
know right from wrong,
But you turn from good, and for evil long.

You destroy my people, chopping them up
like meat for the cooking pot.
To beg the Lord over your troubles; He
won't even look at your kind of lot.

To you false prophets the Lord says this:
"You lead my people astray; you promise
peace for food, but declare war on those
unable to fulfill your financial wish.

"Night will close around,
And no visions will be found.

"The darkness will cover.
The sun will set on you; your day will be
over!

"Seers will cover in shame their faces,
Diviners filled with disgraces.

"And you will admit
Your messages were not of God, but
counterfeit."

But me. I'm filled with the Lord's spirit
and power, justice and might!
Fearlessly pointing out Israel's sin and
what's not been right!

Listen leaders of Israel, you're hating
justice and twisting all that is right,
Building Jerusalem on a foundation of
murder and the corruptive light.

You govern by bribes, preach only for a
price.
Prophets don't prophesy unless paid; this
is your vice!

You claim upon the Lord you rely.
"No harm can come, for the Lord is among
us," you lie.

Mount Zion will be plowed to just land.
A great forest will grow on the hilltop
where the Temple stands.

Micah 4

The last days will find the Temple of the
Lord in Jerusalem the most important
place on earth.
People from all over will go there to
worship, for all it's worth.

Nations will say, "Let's go to the Temple of
God, to learn His teachings and obey."
For his word will go out from Jerusalem
that day.

The Lord will settle international disputes;
swords will be beaten into plowshares,
spears into pruning hooks.
Wars will stop, military training end, with
all in peace and prosperity, to the Lord
you will forever look.

The Lord says, "I will gather together my
people that day; those who have been
exiles, those filled with grief.
I will make them strong again, and I will
rule from Jerusalem, and be their belief."

O Jerusalem, the citadel of God's people,
your favor and might will return
To Jerusalem will be restored the
kingship, you will learn.

Have you no king to lead? Why are you
screaming in terror?
Have you no wise counselors? Pain has
gripped you like a woman in labor.

You will be sent into exile in Babylon.
Many nations over the years, it is true,
called for your blood and utter
destruction.

But they knew not the Lord's thoughts
and plan, then,
To gather those nations together and to
the ground be trampled and beaten.

The Lord says, " Rise and destroy the
nations, with bronze hooves and iron
horns.
Trample to pieces the nations, and give all
wealth as offerings to me, the One to
adorn."

Micah 5

Be alert with your troops! Jerusalem is
under siege with a rod to strike the
leader's face.
O Bethlehem Ephrathah, small village,
you are to be Israel leader's home base.

Abandoned to enemies will you be until
the son's birth through tough labor.
Then fellow countrymen will return from
exile to live undisturbed.

He will lead his flock in the majesty of the
Lord God,
The source of our peace, honored the
world over where we trod.

When the Assyrians invade,
We'll appoint seven rulers to watch over us
and eight princes to lead the charade.

They will rule Assyria with drawn swords,
And rescue us, our reward.

The few left in Israel will go out.
No one will hold back, a strong lion, as the
remnant of Israel goes about.

The people of Israel will stand up to their
foes,
And destroy as the wind blows.

"At the same time," says the Lord, "I will
destroy every weapon,
Demolish walls and defenses; stop idol
worship and witchcraft, the likes against
heaven.

"I'll abolish pagan shrines and all things
worshipped made by your hand.
I will demolish cities where your idol
temples stand.

"You will see
My vengeance poured out on all nations
refusing to obey me."

Micah 6

Listen to what the Lord says:
"Stand up, state your case against me. Let
the mountains be witness.

"Now listen as the Lord complains.
He'll prosecute to the fullest extent for
who's to blame.

"Why have you turned from Me? I brought
you out of slavery.
I sent Moses, Aaron, and Miriam, all three
for their willingness and bravery.

"Remember King Balak of Moab trying to
have you cursed?
But Balaam, son of Boer, what he did was
a blessing, the reverse?

"The journey from Acacia to Gilgal
When I did teach you how not to fall?"

For this, what should we do?
Offer yearling calves; thousands of rams;
rivers of oil; or the firstborn child to get
sins cleansed through and through?

No, the Lord has said how to trod.
Do what is right, love mercy, and walk
humbly with God.

Listen, and fear the Lord those who are
wise!
"Getting rich by cheating; treasures gained
by dishonesty, extortion and violence; and
lying untruths his voice cries!

"I will bring you to ruin for your sins, all.
You will eat but still have pangs; you'll
never have enough money; and the money
saved will go to conquerors as you fall.

"Planted crops won't be harvested; pressed
olives won't be enough to anoint and
shine.
The grapes you trample won't produce
enough for your wine.

"The evil King Omri's laws are the only
ones you keep.
King Ahab's life is the example you keep.

"Thus, you will be ruined, in complete,
And all who see you, with contempt will
treat."

"Thou shalt sow, but thou shalt not reap."—Micah vi. 15.

Micah 7

Misery is mine!
I feel like a fruit picker after harvest with
nothing to find.

The godly people have left, leaving only
murderers,
Who set traps for their own brothers.

Demanding bribes, officials and judges
team,
Using money and influential people to
scheme.

Even the best is like a brier, and judgment
day is nearer.
Even the straightest are crooked, and time
of punishment is here.

Trust no one, neither your best friend nor
your wife.
The son despises the father, the daughter,
the true love of his life.

Daughter-in-law will defy mother-in-law,
bold,
And your enemies will be right in your
own household.

For me, I look to the Lord for help,
Awaiting confidently he'll hear my yelp.

Though I fall and sit in darkness with all
my sin,
The Lord will be my light to rise again.

With patience for punishment must I wait,
For my sins against him, but then the
stories I relate.

The evil my enemies have brought against
me,
Only then his righteousness will I see

My enemies will then see that the Lord is
on my side.
Ashamed, they'll ask, "Where is the Lord,
the God in whom you abide?"

I'll see them trampled down,
Like mud into the ground.

Israel's cities will be rebuilt and mended,
With its borders extended.

Many people will come and honor to you
deliver,
From Assyria to Egypt, and from Egypt to
the Euphrates River.

They'll come from distant seas and every
mountain.
But empty and desolate because of
wickedness will become of the land.

O Lord, come and rule! Lead your flocks in
pastures like they long ago had.

Help them live in peace and prosperity,
enjoying fertile pastures of Bashan and
Gilead.

"Yes," says the Lord, "I'll do miracles for
you,
Like the slavery in Egypt I helped you
through."

The nations of the world will stand in awe
and cower
To the embarrassment felt by their
insignificant power.

What lowly creatures they'll realize they
are.
At his meeting, stand with fear and
trembling terror.

No other God like you pardons sins and
survivors
And you can't stay angry against your
people forever.

Once again you will have compassion,
Trampling under foot and tossing our sins
into depths of the ocean.

Your faithfulness and unfailing love will
you show,
Just as you promised Abraham and Jacob
long ago.

The Book of Nahum.ipp

Nahum 1

The Lord, a jealous God, takes revenge on
those who oppose him.
This is seen by message concerning
Nineveh through Nahum.

He destroys enemies, never letting the
guilty go.
At His command, He displays power over
storm and whirlwind, blow.

Oceans and rivers dry up, and the
pastures fade.
Forests wilted are made.

Mountains quake, and hills melt away.
Who stands against this burning fury?

The Lord is good, a strong refuge.
Enemies are pursued into the night, and
swept away by floods, huge.

What's with all the scheming?
You must be dreaming!

With one blow, He can destroy you.
He won't need two!

Enemies like straw will burn,
So when will your king, plotting against
the Lord, learn?

The Lords says, though with many allies,
The Assyrians will be completely destroyed
and tossed aside.

My people have learned the punishment
lesson,
So I won't let them again suffer under
Assyrian oppression.

To the Assyrians in Nineveh, the Lords
says, your names will be made void,
As future children and all idols in temples
to your gods will be destroyed.

I am preparing graves,
For you all are the dirtiest knaves.

A messenger with good news comes over
the mountains
Peace and celebration, for your enemies of
Nineveh are the object of destruction.

Nahum 2

Armies already surround Nineveh. Man
your defenses for the attack to begin,
For Israel lies broken and empty, but the
Lord will restore its power and honor
again.

Shields are red from being sunlit;
uniforms scarlet.
Swiftly racing recklessly down city streets
are many a-chariot.

Set defenses, the king orders; but officers
stumble in haste.
Too late! Gates are open to let flood-waters
in, and the palace is about to be put to
waste.

Like moaning doves, servant girls mourn
of reservoirs, leaking;
People are slipping away, running, still,
through all the shrieking.

Loot the silver, and plunder the gold,
For uncounted wealth does Nineveh's
treasure in there to behold.

In empty shambles, hearts melt in horror
and knees shake.
People stand aghast, faces pale and
quake.

So now lion of Nineveh, are you bold,
Where nothing was to fear between the
young and old?

You crushed enemies all under,
Filling your city with captives and
plunder.

Now, I am your biggest non-fan!
With chariots up in smoke, you will be left
to not plunder again.

Nahum 3

How terrible, city of deceit and murdering
cries,
Nineveh, in which much to be plundered
lies.

Listen to cracking whips, rumbling wheels,
and pounding hooves; see the flashing
sword,
The glittering spears, and the streets filled
with the many dead of the human horde.

A pretty but faithless city,
Nineveh enticed nations to false gods with
its enchanting beauty.

"No wonder I am your enemy," declares
the Lord Almighty,
"You're deserved of treacherous plenty.

"The world will see your nakedness and
shame,
The vile filth of which you are to blame.

"All who see you in this way,
Nineveh lies in utter ruins, is what they'll
say.

"None will have any interruption,
Nor regret your timely destruction."

Thebes fell, yet surrounded by water,
helped and supported by Put and Libya,
Egypt and Ethiopia,

Nations, which gave additional strength.
How many days do you expect to add to
your city's longevity and length?

Thebes fell, captives taken away, babies
dashed on the streets to death,
Soldiers casting lots for the officers to
servants breath.

You, too, will stagger like a drunkard.
Even those, too, who hid down, hunkered.

For fortresses will fall like figs into mouths
at every turn.
Troops will be weak, gates open for the fire
to burn.

Get ready for the siege: make strong the
defenses; make bricks to repair walls.
Trample in the clay and pack in the
molds. But be ready for the fall.

The sword will put you down, fire will you
consume.
Locusts will you strip, though like
grasshoppers, you number and bloom.

Merchants, numbered like stars, have
brought wealth into town,
But like locusts, princes and officials will
help bring the city down.

Assyrian King,
Do hear the ring.

To and fro' scattered are your people.
No shepherd, no healing; the injury is
fatal.

All nations hearing of your annihilation
clap,
As your cruelty found destruction's lap

FALL OF NINEVEH.—Nahum iii

The Book of Habakkuk.ipp

Habakkuk 1

After complaint, Habakkuk received vision
from God.
Through destruction and violence all
around must we trod.

I call for help, for I'm surrounded by folks
who argue and fight.
Laws are useless, paralyzed, injustice
avails. The wicked outnumber those who
do right.

The Lord Almighty said, "Look and be
amazed! Watch and be astounded.
I'm doing things that are unfounded.

"Babylon will be the world's new power.
Across the earth, they will make nations
cower.

"Nothing can stop them, they do as they
may.
Horses swifter than leopards, people fierce
as wolves, like eagles, pouncing their prey.

"Hordes advance like wind in the desert,
scoffing at kings and princes,
Scorning all the defenses.

"Ramps of earth piled against every wall,
But deep guilt, strength, is their sinful
gall."

You are eternal, Holy One.
Have we now your love shunned?

You are just to rise any nation
To correct us from our delineation.

But will you sit idly by
Allowing others destroy those with a more
righteous cry?

Are we but fish caught and killed; creeping
things dragged in nets,
Strung out, object of rejoicing, with their
hoping of successful future conquests?

Habakkuk 2

I'll climb my watchtower now,
And await the answer of God's know-how.

The Lord said, "Write in large, clear letters
on tablet display,
Over time, slowly, steadily, surely, all
things here will be fulfilled without delay.

"The proud trust in self, the way crooked;
wealth is treacherous, the arrogant never
rest.
But the righteous live by faith, doing their
level best.

"Mouths are open wide with greed,
A never satisfied need.

"But a day is coming when
You will get what you deserve for your
extortion and oppression.

"Your debtors will rise, turn and take your
all,
Leaving you helpless and trembling before
your fall.

"Angry lives will be for those you put
under,
You plunderers will be plundered.

"By unjust means you all have gotten rich.
Thinking wealth will buy security, to keep
you families out of the ditch.

"Murders you have committed, shame
brought to your house,
With the stones of the walls, the beams
and ceilings thinking you're a louse.

"Terrible is the building of cities through
murder and corruption,
But the Lord has promised the wealth-to-
ashes destruction.

"Nations have worked hard in vain,
Because time's a-coming when God's glory
will but all to shame.

"You have made neighbors drunk,
But soon will be your time to be a smelly
skunk.

"You come, drink, and be exposed,
As terror will strike because of your
violence and murders now unclosed.

"What is gained by idols, man-made,
Where foolish trust is laid?

"You beg a lifeless wooden idol to save
you,
You ask a speechless stone god to tell
what to do."
"Can idols speech be made,
Though with gold and silver over- and
inlaid?

"Lifeless in the inside,
But God in his temple will abide.

"Let the earth before Him be silent,
He upon whom all should be reliant."

" I will stand upon my watch, and set me upon
the tower."-- *Hab.* ii. 1.

Habakkuk 3

I have heard all about you,
Filled with awe of the amazing things you
do.

In the time of need, begin
As you did years gone by, help us again.

Use your power to save us
But in your anger, be mercifully gracious.

I see God moving across deserts of Edom
and Pasan,
His brilliant splendor filling the earth and
heaven.

A wonderful god is He,
With rays of light flashing from his hand;
in his awesome power, rejoices He.

Where plague follows him close behind,
In front pestilence marches is what one
would find.

He stops, and the earth shakes.
He looks, the nations quake.

He shatters everlasting mountains, leaving
hills level.
His power is not diminished and not from
the devil!

Peoples of Cushan
Tremble in terror like those of Midian

In anger, Lord, were you displeased
When you struck the river and parted the
seas?

No! But with sensation,
You were sending chariots of salvation.

With commanding power,
You split open the earth with rivers, like
opening the petals of a flower.

Onward the raging waters swept
With hands lifted to the Lord, the mighty
deep wept.

The lofty sun and moon began to fade
By brilliance your arrows and your
flashing spears made.

You marched across the land in anger,
Knowing the nations were in much
danger.
You went to rescue your people, chosen
To save the anointed ones.

You laid bare the bones
Crushing heads of the wicked like stone.

You have had your day
With those thinking Israel would be easy
prey.

With your horses you trampled the sea,
And have piled high the waters, mighty.

With fear, my legs tremble with terror; my
lips quiver,
But I'll wait until you will deliver.

Though no grapes are on the vine, nor
blossoms upon the fig tree,
And the olive crops fail, the fields barren
and empty,

I will rejoice in the Lord, God of my
Salvation.
With strength, swiftness of foot, and safety
over the mountains will be revelation.

To the choir director, to be accompanied
by instruments, strung,
This prayer by Habakkuk, sung.

The Book of Zephaniah.ipp

Zephaniah 1

Zephaniah received these messages when
Josiah was king of Judah.
He was the great-great grandson of
Hezekiah.

"Everything in all your land, I will sweep
leaving no trace," says the Lord,
"Both animals and those of the human
race.

"Fish in the sea will die,
As will all birds of the sky.

"The wicked, I will reduce to rubble,"
(As a beard is whacked to just stubble.)

"Both Judah and Jerusalem with my fist
will they be destroyed,
Every last evidence of Baal worship made
void.

"Those who worship me no more will be
put to an end, to include every idolatrous
priest.
Even they claim to follow the Lord, but
only later make me their least."

Stand in silence for the Lord's Day of
judgment has come.
A great slaughter prepared, leaders and
princes of Judah and all those of pagan
customs.

"The participants of a pagan ceremony
who steal and kill
For their masters home with loot do fill.

"On that day from the Fish Gate will alarm
come
And echo throughout the Misneh section.

"For the surrounding hills, a great
crashing sound will come.
Wailing in sorrow those of the market area
will to death succumb.

"I will search all corners for the sin-
contented and the indifferent who only
whine.
Those whose homes will be plundered and
ransacked, the very ones to never live in
new homes built nor drink of the new
wine.

"The terrible day is near, when strong men
will bitterly pout;
The day when the Lord's anger will be
poured out.

"It is a day of rain, destruction, distress
and gloom,
A day the trumpet calls and battle cries,
as walled cities and fortresses go down in
doom.

"Because against the Lord you have
sinned,
You'll be made helpless as a blind man."

"Your blood will be poured upon the
earth's crust,
Your bodies lying and rotting in the
ground and dust."

Your silver and gold will be no longer
useful as you may
On this, the angry Lord's Day!

A jealous-riddled fire to devour will he
send,
Making for a terrifying end.

Zephaniah 2

You shameless nations, while there is
time, gather together and pray.
Do so before judgment begins and
opportunity is blown away.

Act now!
Bow.

Beg the Lord to save you. Those who walk
humbly and do what is right.
Maybe even then on that day, you'll be
protected in his sight.

Gaza, Ashkelon, Ashod, and Ekron will be
rooted and left in desolation.
Along the coast and in Canaan, you, too,
prepare for destruction.

No on will remain,
Save the few survivors of Judah who will
have prosperity again.

For they will lie in rest in abandoned
Ashkelon.
And the Lord will visit these people of
whom he's fond,

"Taunts of the people of Moab and Ammon
have been heard in horror.
Thus, both will be destroyed like Sodom
and Gomoreh.

"Sting nettles, salt pits, and eternal
desolation will be of their land.
My people left to plunder, that's my plan!"

They will see wages of their pride,
For they scoff at ones whom in the Lord
abide.

The Lord will terrify them and destroy all
gods in the land.
Then nations around the world will see
that heaven's Lord is grand.

"You Ethiopians will be slaughtered by the
sword,"
Lands north, Assyria (Nineveh) will be the
fist strike of the Lord.

Nineveh, a once boisterous proud city of
much stature,
Will become a desolate wasteland for
sheep and cattle to have pasture.

No greater city in the world was there,
Now in ruins, a place of derisive laughter
and the defiant stare.

"Sing, O daughter of Zion."—*Zeph.* iii 14.

Zephaniah 3

Jerusalem, a city of violence and crime,
very polluted and rebellious,
Has become very hellacious.

It refuses to do what it must,
That is to God draw near or in the Lord
trust.

The leaders are lions hunting for all in
their hands can lay;
The judges like ravenous wolves leaving by
morning no trace of their prey;

Priests defile and disobey;
And prophets just lie away.

But the Lord is there, and he is not to be
blamed.
No one takes notice of his justice – the
wicked know no shame.

"I have wiped out nations, complete
devastation.
Cities now desolated, streets in silent ruin
and no witnesses within the population.

"'Surely,' I thought, 'they will revere.'
But no! They continue in their ways
without fear.

"They continue their evil, sinful ways,
Dawn to dusk, and dusk to dawn,
unfazed.

"The time will soon come; be patient,
When I'll stand and accuse each and every
evil nation.

"It's my decision
To gather all nations together and destroy
with my jealous fire contemplation.

"As lips will be purified that day,
So everyone will be together to worship
and pray.

"My people beyond rivers of Ethiopia
Will present their offerings, unafraid, for
they'll be in a utopia.

"Rebels against me you will not be again.
The proud and arrogant will not be on my
holy mountain.

"The people surviving will trust in the
Lord, doing no wrong to each other,
Never telling lies or deceiving one another.

"Peaceful lives, not afraid to sleep.
With no one around, they'll be able this
life to keep."

Israel shouts; Zion's daughter sings.
The Lord will remove the judgment and
disperse your enemies, and come to live
among you as Israel's king.

At last, trouble will be over, fear and
disorder no more.
The announcement will be, "Clean up, the
Lord your God will live among your shore."

He will rejoice over you as almighty savior,
all fears to calm.
He will exult over you by singing a happy
song.

"I will gather those who mourn; not to be
disgraced anymore.
To those who have oppressed you, I am
surely sore.

"The weak, helpless and those chased
away will be saved,
Giving glory and renown to my former
exiles once to ridicule-enslaved.

"They have been mocked and shamed.
On that day, I gather you together and
then bring home again with a good name.

"They'll praise you as I restore before their
eyes your fortunes,
I, the Lord, have spoken."

The Book of Haggai.ipp

"Then spake Haggai the
Lord's messenger."
—*Hag.* i. 13.

C. J. STANILAND.

Haggai 1

On August 29ᵗʰ, 520 B.C., as on official
record,
Through Haggai came a message from the
Lord.

To Zerubbabel, of Shealtiel, Judah
governor, and to Jeshua, son of high
priest Jehozadak,
The Lord's saying, The people say it's not
time to build the Temple back.

The Lord sent message through Haggai,
"You live in luxury, but my house is in
ruins. Why?

"Think about how things are going.
Much has been planted, but the harvest
winds haven't been blowing.

"You're with plenty of food to eat,
But you remain unfilled down to your feet.

"Wine plentiful is for you to drink,
But not enough to satisfy what you think.

"Clothing is there to wear,
But you're still a warm-less bare.

"Your wages and pay
Pass through pockets in only a day.

"Think how things are going.
Go into the hills, bring timber and rebuild
my house, knowing

"I'd in it take pleasure,
Then you'd have all your treasure.

"For rich harvests you had hoped,
Not the poor with which doped.

"And when to home your harvest came,
I blew it away again. I'm to blame.

"But my house in ruins lies,
While you remain busy building to the
skies.

"Drought was called to withhold the dew,
As the earth the crops dried and withdrew.

"A drought to whither the olives and grain,
And your hard-earned everything to ruin
and drain."

The whole remnant of God's people
obeyed, those who were told why,
The message from the Lord's messenger,
Haggai:

"I'm with you,"
Sparking words of enthusiasm for the
building of the Temple be through.

The work on the Temple was to begin
On September 21st of King Darius' reign.

Haggai 2

Then on October 17, another message
through Haggai was sent
To all God's people is where it went.

Is there any from before who knew the
Temple,
How it compares now; it just might be
simple.

Take courage people still left in the land,
For I'm still in charge of the plan.

My Spirit remains, so don't be afraid.
Just as out of Egypt I led, I also had this
plan laid.

The Lord Almighty says, "I will shake the
earth and heavens,
The oceans and dry land, and also all the
nations.

"The treasures of all will come to the
Temple.
I will fill it with glory, all gold and all
silver. It's all mine and rather simple.

"Future glories will be greater to last,
Than those of the glorious past.

"And in this place, peace will be forever its
token.
For I, the Lord Almighty, has spoken."

December 18th of the same year
Brought another question to answer clear.

"Of the priests was asked,
"If one carrying a holy sacrifice brushes
against anything, does it become holy
unmasked?'

'No!' the priests stated.
But God, through Haggai, was berated.

What if one becomes ceremonially
unclean,
By touching death and upon the things
refined, lean.

Will it be defiled?
"Yes," the priests smiled!

Then said Haggai, That's how it is with
this nation compiled.
Everything done and all things offered is
defiled.

"Think of things going on.
Before you began laying the foundation.

"Hoped for twenty-bushel crop
But to 10 did it drop.

"You expected 50 gallons from the
winepress,
But 20 was found after this time of
duress.

"All produce of your labor fail,
Yet, you still to me did not hail!

"So on the 18th day
When the Lord's Temple foundation lay,

"I promise while seed is in barn still,
before the harvest of grain, or before the
grapevine, or trees of fig, olive or
pomegranate,
You will be the most blessed of me on this
planet!"

A second message of the 18th went,
When to tell Zerubbabel it was sent.

"I'll overthrow royal thrones, destroying
foreign powers, as I'm about the earth to
shake
The heavens and earth, and with changes
to make.

"Horses will fall, riders killing each other,
When chariots turnover.

"I will honor you then, Zerubbabel, my
servant,
Giving a ring signet.

"One specially for you chosen.
I, the Lord, has spoken."

The Book of Zechariah.ipp

Zechariah 1

Of the second year of King Darius' reign,
in about mid-autumn,
A message to Zechariah did come.

"I, the Lord, with your ancestors am very
upset.
Thus, tell the people so they will not
regret.

"Return to me, and I'll return to you,
Unlike your ancestral crew.

"Don't be like them, who wouldn't listen to
earlier prophets,
When the Lord Almighty said, 'Turn from
evil ways and for evil practices to stop it.'

"Now those ancestors and prophets are
long dead,
And all things happened as I have said.

"As a result, they repented,
And they said, 'Deserved are we what the
Lord upon us presented.'"

Another message sent to the prophet
Zechariah,
Grandson of Iddo, son of Berekiah.

This happened February 15,
B.C. 519.

Zechariah said, "The vision during the night,
A man sitting upon a red horse behind myrtle trees was in the sight.

"And behind him more other horses, red, brown and white.
So about the horses I asked the angel to shed me some light."

The angel replied, "I will show,
So you will know."

The man among the trees stated,
"They are the ones out to patrol and have the earth rated."

And to the angel of the Lord, they reported,
"The whole world is at peace," they retorted.

At hearing this, the angel of the Lord prayed:
"For 70 years you've been angry with Jerusalem and Judah; how long until mercy upon them is laid?"

The Lord spoke kind, comforting words to the angel who spoke with me,
"Shout a message for all to hear: 'My love for Jerusalem and Mount Zion is strong, but I'm angry at those who enjoy peace and security.

'I was with my people angry for only a little
redirection,
But those other nations sent to punish
went far beyond my expectation.'

"This, then, is what says the Lord.
"I return to show mercy, my Temple to
rebuild, and the Jerusalem reconstruction
board."

Then looking up to see animal horns, four,
I asked of the angel, "What are these for?"

"The horns represent world powers," he
spattered,
"Judah, Israel, and Jerusalem, scattered."

The Lord showed four blacksmiths.
I asked, "What do they wish?"

The blacksmiths have come to terrify the
horns,
The ones scattering and humbling Judah,
will be destroyed with scorn.

" I saw by night, and behold a man riding upon a red horse."
—*Zech.* i. 8.

Zechariah 2

I looked up again to see a man with a
measuring line in his hand,
When asked about it, he replied, I'm
measuring width and length of Jerusalem
land."

The angel with me went to meet another
one,
Who said, "Tell the young man Jerusalem
will be so full there won't be enough room
for everyone.

"Many will live outside the walls, yet safe
will it be.
I will be the wall of fire around," says the
Lord, "and inside the city, glory."

Says the Lord, "Flee from the North and
the four winds to which scattered, escape
to Jerusalem you whoa are exiled in
Babylon,"
And after the period of glory, "Anyone who
harms you harms my most precious
possession."

"To know I was sent by the Lord
Almighty," he says, "My fist will I raise to
put them under,
Leaving their slaves to plunder."

Says the Lord, "Shout and rejoice,
Jerusalem, for I am coming to live among
you.
Many nations will join themselves, and
they will be my people, too."

Jerusalem chosen as his own city, Judah's
land will be the Lord's inheritance.
All humanity, be silent before the Lord, for
he's springing into action from his holy
residence.

Zechariah 3

The angel showed me the high priest
Jeshua,
Hebrew variation of Joshua,

Before the Lord being accused by Satan of
many things.
But to the Lord nothing rings.

The Lord said to Satan, "I reject your
accusations, rebuking" (the liar).
"This man is like a burning stick pulled
from a fire."

Jeshua's clothing was in a dirty way,
So the angel said to another, "Take off and
throw these away."

To Jeshua, he said, "I take away your sins,
And with new you are given."

Then I said, "Could a new turban be put
upon his head high?"
So a clean one was put on his head while
the angel of the Lord stood by.

Then very solemnly did the angel speak:
"The Lord says
'You will be given authority over my
Temple, walk in my presence, if you follow
my ways and requirements.

"Listen, Jeshua and other priests, "You
are symbols of things to come.

The jewel before Jeshua, a single stone
with seven facets, I will engrave an
inscription.

My servant, the Branch, I soon will bring,
In a single day, I'll remove sins of the land.
Here's the final thing:

"On that day," says the Lord Almighty,
"You each will invite neighbors into your
home to share peace and prosperity."

"Not by might, nor by power, but by my Spirit, saith the Lord of hosts."
—Zech. iv. 6.

Zechariah 4

The angel who'd been talking returned and
woke me,
"What do you now see?"

I answered, "A lampstand, solid gold, with
a bowl of oil on it.
Around it are seven lamps, each with
seven spouts and a matching wick.

"Also, one on each side of the bowl, I see,
An olive tree."

I asked the angel, "What does this mean,
These things I have seen?"

Asked the angel, "Don't you know?"
My reply was, "My lord, no."

He then gave account
Of what this was about.

Then to me he began to rattle
"This is what the Lord said to Zerubbabel:"

"By my spirit, and not by strength nor by
force,
All will flatten before him, but nothing will
stand blocking Zerubbabel's course.

Zerubbabel will set in place the Temple's
final stone,
And the people's "May God bless it!" verses
will be thrown.

Then another message from the Lord came
to me,
"Zerubbabel laid the foundation of this
Temple, and completing it will be he.

"The Lord, you will know, has sent me,
Don't despise the small beginnings, it's the
beginning the Lord rejoices to see,

"And to see the plumb line in Zerubbabel's
hand,
For these seven lamps, representing the
eyes of the Lord, search all the earth's
land."

I asked the angel, then
"What are the two olive trees on each side
of the lamp stand,

The two branches that pour out through
The golden oil of the gold tubes?"

The angel replied, "Don't you know?"
I replied, "My lord, no."

Then he said, "They represent (their
worth),
Two anointed ones who assist the Lord of
all the earth."

Zechariah 5

Again I looked up to see a scroll flying.
"What did you see?" the angel replying.

"I see a flying scroll," I replied,
"30 feet long and 15 feet wide."

"The scroll contains," the angel said,
"what's going on throughout the land:
'Those who steal will be forever banned.'"

"The other side says those who falsely
swear
will be also banished from everywhere."

"Into the house of the thief and everyone
who swears falsely by my name,
Until the house is completely destroyed –
timber and stones – my curse will remain."

Then the angel said, "Look up, as
something appears in the sky."
"what is it?" asked I.

"It is a basket," he said, "for measuring
grain,
"Filled with sins of the vain."

Off the basket was lifted a heavy lead
cover.
A woman sitting inside was named
"Wickedness," and the lid was pulled over.

I looked up to see two women with wings
to fly.
Their wings. like a stork's, picked up the
basket into the sky.

"Where are they taking it?" of the angel
asked I.
"To Babylonia where a Temple will be
built," did he reply.

"When the Temple is ready,
Upon its pedestal will it be placed, steady."

" And behold a flying roll."—*Zech.* v. 1.

Zechariah 6

I looked up again and four chariots with
horses pulling did I see.
Red, black, white, and dappled-gray
horses. "What are these?" I asked the
angel with me.

"These, the four spirit winds of heaven, go
out to do what comes from the Lord's
mouth.
The black horse-drawn chariot is going
North, white West, and gray South.

The powerful horses were eager to be off,
As the Lord said, "Patrol the earth, get
aloft."

The Lord then told me,
"Those going North, vent my spirit, angry."

I received, then, another message of things
to behold.
"Of Heldai, Tobijah, and Jedaiah, will
bring exiled Babylonian gold.

"Make a crown and put on Jeshua's head,
And to him what the Lord has said.

The man called The Branch here stands,
And all will happen if you carefully obey
the Lord's commands.

He'll build the Lord's Temple, receiving
royal honor to as a king upon his throne.

There'll be a priest by his side, and the
two together in harmony hone.

The crown a memorial to those who save it
– Heldai, Tobijah, Jedaiah,
And Josiah, son of Zephaniah.

Many will come to rebuild from distant
lands,
And at this, you'll know it's all from the
Lord Almighty's hands.

Zechariah 7

On December 7, B.C.518, another
message to Zechariah came.
The people of Bethlehem sent Sharezer
and Regemmelech, the prophets and
princes of the Temple an answer to a
question to determine.

"Shall we continue to mourn the
anniversary of the Temple's destruction,
Just as we have for years done?"

From the Lord, this message upon me did
fall.
"Say to peoples and princes, all,

"During the 70 years of exile during
mourning and fasting,
Was it for me, the Lord everlasting?"

"For during your festival time even now,
You think not about me, even to give the
simplest bow.

"Isn't this the same message related
Years ago when Judah and Negev were
quite populated?"

Then a message to Zechariah: The Lord
says, "Judge fairly and treat others the
same, showing mercy and kindness to one
another.

Don't oppress widows, orphans,
foreigners, and the poor; don't make evil
plans to harm each other.

"Your ancestors wouldn't listen, with
hatred and not listening to the law.
This was their flaw.

"I refused, as they did, to listen,
And I scattered them to many a-nation.

"Their land became so desolate,
As a desert from once being so pleasant."

Zechariah 8

Another message did come to me
From the Lord Almighty.

He says: "My love for Mt. Zion is
passionate and strong.
I am consumed by Jerusalem.

"I'm returning to Mt. Zion to live in
Jerusalem where it may.
Called Faithful City, once again old men
and women will walk the streets filled with
boys and girls at play.

"Though this may seem impossible to you,
but not to me,
You small discouraged remnant of God's
people; why think it not possible for the
Lord Almighty?

"I'll rescue my people from the East and
West,
To bring them home to live safely in
Jerusalem's nest.

"My people then must
And I, their God, will be just.

"The Lord says: take heart and listen
To the prophets whistling.

"The building of the Temple of God, since
the foundation was laid,
No jobs existed, no wages paid.

"No traveler was safe, enemies on each side.
I turned everyone against each other as they abide.

"But now I'm planting seeds of prosperity and peace,
Allowing crops to produce and the sky, the dew release.

"Judah and Jerusalem became symbols of the cursed,
But now they are a blessing source.

"So don't be discouraged or afraid,
But on with the rebuilding where the Temple is laid.

"I did not change my mind about your ancestors and my anger.
I promised the punishment danger.

"Neither will I forget to bless,
But with resolute redress.

"Tell the truth; courts verdicts should be just;
Make not evil plans; false swearing to stop is a must.

"Don't wait.
These things, I hate.

"Traditional fasts and times of mourning
during seasons must now cease.
Instead, have festivals of joy, loving truth
and peace.

"People of nations around the world to
Jerusalem will travel,
Seeking the Lord Almighty's blessings in
lives unraveled.

"Clutching the Jew's robe on the side,
Saying, "Let us walk with you, for in you
God does abide!"

" And they shall devour, and subdue with sling-stones."—*Zech.* ix. 15.

Zechariah 9

This message is from the Lord to the land
of Aram and the city of Damascus,
For all eyes of humanity upon the Lord
will focus.

Doom is certain for Hamath, Sidon, and
Tyre,
Cities thinking that they are clever.

As common as dust is the silver and gold
piled in Tyre,
But the Lord will strip away, and burn to
the ground with fire.

Ashkelon will see Tyre fall and be filled
with fear,
But will be destroyed, completely and
shear.

With dashed hopes, Gaza and Ekron will
shake with terror,
Gaza's king killed and its people
conquered.

Foreigners will occupy Ashdod, and I'll
destroy the pride of the Philistines.
No longer will they eat meat with blood in
it, nor other foods forbidden.

Surviving Philistines will worship our god,
Allah,
And will become a leader in Judah.

I will guard my Temple, protecting it from
every invading army.
I'm watching their movements; no foreign
oppressor will again cause disharmony.

O people of Zion, shout in triumph.
Rejoice greatly.
Your king is coming, righteous and
victorious, yet humble, riding on a donkey.

Battle chariots will be removed from
battle,
And I'll destroy all weapons used in battle.

Your king will bring nations peace.
His realm from sea to sea, and to the ends
of the earth from the River Euphrates.

The covenant I made with you, sealed by
blood, gives all you prisoners hope.
Come back to the safety slope.

I promise this very day,
Two mercies for each woe will I repay.

Brandishing like a warrior, Israel my
arrow and Jerusalem my sword, Judah
will be my bow,
The Greeks will know it so!

Above his people will the Lord appear,
Protecting them, not allowing his enemies
near.

They will subdue their enemies with stone,
And they will shout in battle as being
drunk to the bone.

When the day arrives, like jewels in a
crown the people will shine,
And they will thrive on abundance of grain
and new wine.

Zechariah 10

It is the Lord who makes the skies flush,
Dropping showers of rain to fields become
pastures, lush.

My people wander like lost sleep,
False gods give false advice, fortune-tellers
not the truth peep.

I burn with anger against your shepherds,
And I will punish these leaders.

For the Lord has arrived to look after his
flock,
Making them of warhorse stock.

"I will strengthen Judah and save Israel. I
hear their cries, for they are mine.
Mighty warriors will they become, their
hearts happy as of wine.

When I whistle, they'll come running,
And to its former size will I redeem their
population.

Still they remember me while scattered in
distant land,
With their children, they will survive and
come home again.

"Through the sea of distress will they
pass, Egyptian rule end and Assyrian
pride broken.

I will make my people strong in my power,
giving all they wish, the Lord has spoken."

Zechariah 11

Open your doors, Lebanon, through which
cedar forests fire sweep.
For all ruined cedars, beautiful and tall,
cypress trees weep.

Oaks of Bashan, thickest forests fell,
For lost and gone wealth, the shepherds
wail.

The Lord my God says: "Care for a flock
meant for slaughter.
About the slaughter, buyers have no
remorse and sellers say, "I'm rich with
shoulders halter."

"Likewise, I will have pity no longer on the
inhabitants of the land,
 Letting them fall into each other's
clutches and into the clutches of the
king's hand."

I cared for the flock, oppressed, for
slaughter the one intended.
Two staffs I took, named Favor and Union,
and three evil shepherds I ended.

But I became impatient with these sheep –
this nation.
Hating me, too, I stated, "I won't be their
shepherd any longer," without hesitation.

"If you die, you die; If killed, killed.
Those remaining will be each other's
devouring thrill."

The staff, Favor, I snapped in two, the
nations' covenant revoked.
Those buying and selling sheep watched
as the Lord through me the message
stroked.

And I said to them: "Give my wages,
whatever I'm worth."
They counted out thirty pieces of silver,
which I gave to the treasury.

I then broke in two the other staff, Union,
To show the bond between Israel and
Judah is now broken.

The Lord then said to me: "Go again the
part of a worthless shepherd to play.
An illustration message of a shepherd not
caring for his sheep, I relay.

Doom is certain for such a shepherd, a cut
arm and a pierced right eye.
His arm will be useless, and his right eye
blind!

Zechariah 12

The message from the Lord concerning
Israel's fate:
"He who stretched out the heavens, laid
earth's foundation, and within humans
the spirit make.

"Jerusalem, like an intoxicating drink, will
be like a heavy stone on that day,
And no nation trying to lift it will go
unscathed.

"Every horse will panic, and every rider
will lose his nerve, on that day.
I watch over the people of Judah, blind
enemy horses, and the clans of Judah will
say:

" 'The people of Jerusalem have found
strength
In the Lord Almighty, their God at some
length.'

"Like a brazier setting a woodpile ablaze or
a torch burning among grain, on that day
People in Jerusalem will remain secure,
the clans of Judah will burn nations left
and right as they lay.

Judah victory will be first
So Jerusalem and the royal line of David
will not have greater honor than the rest.

"The weakest will be as mighty as King David, on that day
The Lord will defend Jerusalem's people, pouring out a spirit of power and grace.

On the family of David and on Jerusalem's people,
All the weeping in Israel throughout goes on in ripples.

"The land shall mourn, every family apart." —*Zech.* xii. 12.

Zechariah 13

"On that day opened will be a fountain
For the people of Jerusalem to cleanse of
all sins and defilement.

"Every trace of idol worship will be gotten
rid of on that day.
Every name of idols will be forgotten, the
Lord Almighty did say.

"Those who wear prophet clothes must
now live as a farmer among the land.
Death must come should prophesying be
done again.

"Once boasting the prophetic gift,
Now these must be now an attitude shift.

"Strike down the shepherd, and the sheep
will scatter, O sword.
Two-thirds of the people will die, but the
rest left are mine, says the Lord."

Zechariah 14

On that day, against Jerusalem will be all
the nations,
Plundering in front of you, all your
possessions.

Half the population will be taken captivity;
Half will be left among the ruins of the
city.

The Lord will then go out to fight the
nations.
(He'll do so without hesitation.)

On the Mount of Olives will he stand,
Just as a split comes to the land.

The mountain will split: half will move
north, and half to the south will move.
The valley created is through which you,
as in King Uzziah's days, will groove.

No longer shine will the sources of light.
There will be no normal day, no normal
night.

Flowing continuously in both summer and
winter will the life-giving waters be,
Half flowing toward the Mediterranean and
half toward the Dead Sea.

Over all the earth will the Lord be king,
And to His name alone will be the
worshipping.

All land from Geba will be a plain, to
Rimmon.
Jerusalem will be raised in place, but
inhabited all the way from the Gate,
Benjamin

To the Corner Gate, and from the Tower of
Hananel
To where the king's winepresses fell.

And Jerusalem will be filled, safe at last,
Never again to be cursed or the subject of
a destructive blast.

A plague will be sent to nations against
Jerusalem had fought.
Great malcontent, panic, and terror
stricken will be the lot!

Enemies surviving the plague annually
will go to Jerusalem in the end.
Those nations refusing to go, to them no
rain will the Almighty send!

Cooking pots in Jerusalem and Judah will
be set apart as holy.
Traders that worship day will be no longer
in the Temple of the Lord God Almighty.

The Book of Malachi.ipp

Malachi 1

A message sent to Israel through Malachi
Of the Lord's love without lies,

"My love for you I will not abort,
But you retort,

"'How has this love been?'
It started way back with Jacob, your kin.

Though rejected I Esau and turned into
desert his inheritance,
Rebuilding after the destruction may be
done by descendents.

But the Lord simply may say
Though they rebuild, I'll again demolish
their country where it may lay.

The Land of the Wickedness as by decree,
Will inhabit the people with which God is
forever angry.

When you see the destructed blank slate,
You'll say the Lord's power is truly great!

To priests, He says, "A son honors and a
master will be served.
But I, your Father and master, has not
what is deserved.

"You have despised my name.
No need to have asked what was to blame.

"Defiled sacrifices upon my altar.
'How?' you ask. "By giving blind, diseased,
crippled animals is how I find fault.

"Is it not wrong to do such a thing?
Try giving these to the governor –and he
isn't even a king!

"So to God, beg.
I shall any favor renege.

"My wish is for one to close the door.
The temple shut to receive your faulty
offerings no more.

"I am not with you pleased,
The way you have teased.

"People of all nations around the world
honor me with offerings,
Sweet incense and pure things."
"Food contemptible
Brought to the Lord's table?

"You turn up noses at his every command,
So upon you is where any consequences
land.

"Think of it!
What's given me are stolen, cripple, and
sick.

"Cursed is one who promises a fine ram
but to God a defective one fling.
Feared by all the nations, I am a great
king!"

Malachi 2

Listen priests to this command.
Take to heart, all of you throughout the
land.

Honor my name,
Or a terrible curse will be brought with
you to blame.

My warnings you do not heed.
Your blessings are already cursed, indeed.

Let me give you the highlights:
So at last you'll know who sent this
warning about my covenant with the
Levites.

I'll rebuke your descendents, splatter your
faces with dung of sacrifices, adding you
to the dung heap.
It'll be a time to weep.

The purpose of the covenant was the life
and peace thing.
And reverence and awe of my name did
they bring!

They passed on to the people truth; didn't
lie or cheat.
They walked with me, and from sin helped
many others to retreat.

Priests lips should guard knowledge,
receiving messages for instruction.

You have left the path, and have caused
many to stumble towards destruction.

The Levites covenant is among your guilty
affiliation,
Leading to your being despised and world-
wide humiliation.

Aren't we all created and of the same God
and Father?
Then why so much faithlessness to each
other?

In Judah, Israel, and Jerusalem, there
exists treachery,
Men marrying idol-worshipping women,
and defiling the Lord's sanctuary.

May the Lord cut off from the nation every
man doing these things,
Yet an offering to the Lord brings.

You're weeping, groaning and covering the
Lord's altar with tears,
Crying out, "Why has the Lord let us with
abandoning fears?"

I'll tell you, as it is the vow.
Disloyalty to your wife, your wonderful
wow!

God made you two one,
So never each other shun.

For I hate divorces, the Lords says.
Remain loyal, and guard where your
loyalty lays.

With your words have you the Lord
wearied.
"How," you ask. "Where is the Lord of
Justice?" too many times queried.

" Bring ye all the tithes into the storehouse."—*Mal* iii. 10.

Malachi 3

"I'm sending a message to prepare the
way.
The Lord you seek will come to his Temple
that day."

The messenger for whom you look for
eagerly,
Is surely coming, but do wait not so
leisurely.

Like a blazing fire that refines metal,
Or a strong soap that cleanses clothes
where dirt may settle,

He will sit and judge like refining silver of
dross.
(He, you must not cross.)

He will purify the Levites, making them
again respectable,
And they will offer sacrifices again
acceptable.

Once more will He accept offerings of the
Judah and Jerusalem people,
Those strong standing trials and not so
feeble.

I will stand witness against all sorcerers,
Even against all liars and adulterers.

Those who cheat on paying wages,
Who oppress widows and orphans, or
those depriving justice to foreigners
through ages.

These people do not fear me!
Says the Lord, "Hear me!"
I am the Lord, and I don't change,
A reason why you've not been totally
rearranged.

My laws have been scorned and not
obeyed, even by your ancestors.
Return to me, so my love again for you
festers.

Should people cheat God?
No, with a resounding nod!

But you have cheated me by what you do,
Denying tithes and offerings to me due.

Bring enough for me at the Temple, I'll
show you what I can do.
You will see heavens' windows open, a
great blessing will come, enough crops to
see you through.

Against insects and diseases will I guard,
and your grapes will always be ripe.
You will then be called blessed, your land
such a delight.

Against the Lord, terrible things have you
said.
Why serve God, say you, obeying
commands or attempting sins to shed.

You say blessed are the arrogant,
Those doing evil get rich, those who dare
God to punish them then go free from
their predicament.

Then those who feared and loved the Lord
spoke.
The Lord listened, and upon a scroll
someone wrote

Names of these who feared and loved Him
to no measure,
So the Lord Almighty, on that day he acts,
will have his special treasure.

I will spare them as an obedient and
dutiful child.
Then you'll see the difference between the
righteous and the unruly wild,

These who serve God,
And those with the negative nod.

Malachi 4

The Almighty Lord says, judgment day is
coming,
Like a furnace burning.

The arrogant and wicked will be burned
like straw.
They'll be consumed like trees, roots and
all.

For those whom my name fear
Will be like calves let out to pasture, with
freedom near.

On the day I act
You'll tread upon the wicked like dust on
the feet. That's a fact!

Remember obey the instructions
Given Moses while on Mount Sinai, and
other laws and regulations.

Prophet Elijah will be sent before
That great and dreadful day of the Lord.

His preaching will turn hearts, parents to
children, children to parents; love, nothing
worse.
Otherwise, I will come and strike the land
with a curse.

www.ingramcontent.com/pod-product-compliance
Lightning Source LLC
LaVergne TN
LVHW011235080426
835509LV00005B/517